MYSELF,

I LOVE YOU

BECAUSE...

★ *A Daily Journal of Gratitude & Love* ★

NICK KEOMAHAVONG

DEDICATION

This journal is dedicated to anyone needing to selflessly provided support, inspiration, and unconditional love to themselves. Give yourself this gift of loving kindness.

★ *PERSONAL MESSAGE* ★

TO:

FROM:

Date:_____   Day #_____

I LOVE YOU BECAUSE...

_____

_____

_____

_____

_____

_____

_____

_____

_____

_____

_____

_____

_____

Draw the feeling...

_____

_____

_____

Date:_____　　Day #_____

I LOVE YOU BECAUSE...

Draw the feeling...

Date:_____ Day #_____

I LOVE YOU BECAUSE...

Draw the feeling...

Date:_____ Day #_____

I LOVE YOU BECAUSE...

_____

_____

_____

_____

_____

_____

_____

_____

_____

_____

_____

_____

_____

_____

_____

_____

_____

Draw the feeling...

Date:_____   Day #_____

I LOVE YOU BECAUSE...

_____

_____

_____

_____

_____

_____

_____

_____

_____

_____

_____

_____

_____

_____

Draw the feeling...

_____

_____

_____

_____

Date:_____   Day #_____

I LOVE YOU BECAUSE...

Draw the feeling...

Date:_____   Day #_____

I LOVE YOU BECAUSE...

_____

_____

_____

_____

_____

_____

_____

_____

_____

_____

_____

_____

_____

_____

_____

Draw the feeling...

Date:_____ Day #_____

I LOVE YOU BECAUSE...

Draw the feeling...

Date:_____   Day #_____

I LOVE YOU BECAUSE...

_____

_____

_____

_____

_____

_____

_____

_____

_____

_____

_____

_____

_____

_____

_____

_____

_____

Draw the feeling...

_____

Date:_____ Day #_____

I LOVE YOU BECAUSE...

_____

_____

_____

_____

_____

_____

_____

_____

_____

_____

_____

_____

Draw the feeling...

_____

_____

_____

Date:_____   Day #_____

I LOVE YOU BECAUSE...

_____

_____

_____

_____

_____

_____

_____

_____

_____

_____

_____

_____

_____

Draw the feeling...

_____

Date:_____   Day #_____

I LOVE YOU BECAUSE...

_____
_____
_____
_____
_____
_____
_____
_____
_____
_____
_____
_____
_____

Draw the feeling...

Date:_____   Day #_____

I LOVE YOU BECAUSE...

Draw the feeling...

Date:_____ Day #_____

I LOVE YOU BECAUSE...

_____

_____

_____

_____

_____

_____

_____

_____

_____

_____

_____

_____

_____

Draw the feeling...

_____

_____

_____

_____

Date:_____   Day #_____

I LOVE YOU BECAUSE...

_____

_____

_____

_____

_____

_____

_____

_____

_____

_____

_____

_____

_____

_____

Draw the feeling...

_____

Date:_____ Day #_____

I LOVE YOU BECAUSE...

_____
_____
_____
_____
_____
_____
_____
_____
_____
_____
_____
_____
_____
_____
_____
_____
_____

Draw the feeling...

Date:_____ Day #_____

I LOVE YOU BECAUSE...

_____

_____

_____

_____

_____

_____

_____

_____

_____

_____

_____

_____

_____

_____

_____

Draw the feeling...

_____

Date:_____   Day #_____

I LOVE YOU BECAUSE...

Draw the feeling...

Date:_____   Day #_____

I LOVE YOU BECAUSE...

_____
_____
_____
_____
_____
_____
_____
_____
_____
_____
_____
_____
_____
_____

Draw the feeling...

Date:_____   Day #_____

I LOVE YOU BECAUSE...

_____
_____
_____
_____
_____
_____
_____
_____
_____
_____
_____
_____
_____
_____
_____
_____

Draw the feeling...

Date:_____   Day #_____

I LOVE YOU BECAUSE...

_____
_____
_____
_____
_____
_____
_____
_____
_____
_____
_____
_____
_____
_____
_____

Draw the feeling...

Date:_____   Day #_____

I LOVE YOU BECAUSE...

Draw the feeling...

Date:_____ Day #_____

I LOVE YOU BECAUSE...

_____
_____
_____
_____
_____
_____
_____
_____
_____
_____
_____
_____
_____
_____
_____
_____
_____
_____

Draw the feeling...

Date:_____ Day #_____

I LOVE YOU BECAUSE...

Draw the feeling...

Date:_____   Day #_____

I LOVE YOU BECAUSE...

_____

_____

_____

_____

_____

_____

_____

_____

_____

_____

_____

_____

_____

_____

_____

Draw the feeling...

Date:_____   Day #_____

I LOVE YOU BECAUSE...

Draw the feeling...

Date:_____   Day #_____

I LOVE YOU BECAUSE...

Draw the feeling...

Date:_____ Day #_____

I LOVE YOU BECAUSE...

_____
_____
_____
_____
_____
_____
_____
_____
_____
_____
_____
_____
_____
_____
_____

Draw the feeling...

Date:_____ Day #_____

I LOVE YOU BECAUSE...

_____
_____
_____
_____
_____
_____
_____
_____
_____
_____
_____
_____
_____
_____
_____

Draw the feeling...

Date:_____   Day #_____

I LOVE YOU BECAUSE...

Draw the feeling...

Date:_____   Day #_____

I LOVE YOU BECAUSE...

Draw the feeling...

Date:_____ Day #_____

I LOVE YOU BECAUSE...

_____
_____
_____
_____
_____
_____
_____
_____
_____
_____
_____
_____
_____
_____

Draw the feeling...

_____

Date:_____   Day #_____

I LOVE YOU BECAUSE...

_____

_____

_____

_____

_____

_____

_____

_____

_____

_____

_____

_____

_____

_____

Draw the feeling...

_____

Date:_____   Day #_____

I LOVE YOU BECAUSE...

_____
_____
_____
_____
_____
_____
_____
_____
_____
_____
_____
_____
_____

Draw the feeling...

Date:_____   Day #_____

I LOVE YOU BECAUSE...

_____
_____
_____
_____
_____
_____
_____
_____
_____
_____
_____
_____
_____

Draw the feeling...

_____

Date:_____   Day #_____

I LOVE YOU BECAUSE...

Draw the feeling...

Date:_____   Day #_____

I LOVE YOU BECAUSE...

_____
_____
_____
_____
_____
_____
_____
_____
_____
_____
_____
_____
_____
_____

Draw the feeling...

Date:_____   Day #_____

I LOVE YOU BECAUSE...

_____

_____

_____

_____

_____

_____

_____

_____

_____

_____

_____

_____

_____

_____

Draw the feeling...

Date:_____ Day #_____

I LOVE YOU BECAUSE...

_____
_____
_____
_____
_____
_____
_____
_____
_____
_____
_____
_____
_____

Draw the feeling...

Date:_____ Day #_____

I LOVE YOU BECAUSE...

_____

_____

_____

_____

_____

_____

_____

_____

_____

_____

_____

_____

_____

_____

Draw the feeling...

_____

_____

_____

Date:_____   Day #_____

I LOVE YOU BECAUSE...

_____
_____
_____
_____
_____
_____
_____
_____
_____
_____
_____
_____
_____
_____

Draw the feeling...

Date:_____   Day #_____

I LOVE YOU BECAUSE...

Draw the feeling...

Date:_____   Day #_____

I LOVE YOU BECAUSE...

_____

_____

_____

_____

_____

_____

_____

_____

_____

_____

_____

_____

_____

Draw the feeling...

_____

_____

Date:_____   Day #_____

I LOVE YOU BECAUSE...

_____
_____
_____
_____
_____
_____
_____
_____
_____
_____
_____
_____
_____
_____

Draw the feeling...

Date:_____   Day #_____

I LOVE YOU BECAUSE...

_____
_____
_____
_____
_____
_____
_____
_____
_____
_____
_____
_____
_____
_____

Draw the feeling...

_____
_____
_____
_____

Date:_____ Day #_____

I LOVE YOU BECAUSE...

Draw the feeling...

Date:_____   Day #_____

I LOVE YOU BECAUSE...

Draw the feeling...

Date:_____   Day #_____

I LOVE YOU BECAUSE...

_____
_____
_____
_____
_____
_____
_____
_____
_____
_____
_____
_____
_____
_____
_____

Draw the feeling...

Date:_____   Day #_____

I LOVE YOU BECAUSE...

Draw the feeling...

Date:_____   Day #_____

I LOVE YOU BECAUSE...

_____

_____

_____

_____

_____

_____

_____

_____

_____

_____

_____

_____

_____

_____

_____

_____

Draw the feeling...

_____

Date:_____   Day #_____

I LOVE YOU BECAUSE...

Draw the feeling...

Date:_____ Day #_____

I LOVE YOU BECAUSE...

Draw the feeling...

Date:_____   Day #_____

I LOVE YOU BECAUSE...

_____

_____

_____

_____

_____

_____

_____

_____

_____

_____

_____

_____

_____

_____

Draw the feeling...

_____

_____

Date:_____   Day #_____

I LOVE YOU BECAUSE...

_____

_____

_____

_____

_____

_____

_____

_____

_____

_____

_____

_____

_____

_____

_____

_____

_____

Draw the feeling...

Date:_____   Day #_____

I LOVE YOU BECAUSE...

Draw the feeling...

Date:_____ Day #_____

I LOVE YOU BECAUSE...

_____
_____
_____
_____
_____
_____
_____
_____
_____
_____
_____
_____
_____

Draw the feeling...

Date:_____   Day #_____

I LOVE YOU BECAUSE...

_____
_____
_____
_____
_____
_____
_____
_____
_____
_____
_____
_____
_____
_____
_____

Draw the feeling...

Date:_____ Day #_____

I LOVE YOU BECAUSE...

_____

_____

_____

_____

_____

_____

_____

_____

_____

_____

_____

_____

_____

Draw the feeling...

_____

_____

_____

Date:_____ Day #_____

I LOVE YOU BECAUSE...

_____
_____
_____
_____
_____
_____
_____
_____
_____
_____
_____
_____
_____

Draw the feeling...

_____
_____
_____

Date:_____ Day #_____

I LOVE YOU BECAUSE...

Draw the feeling...

Date:_____   Day #_____

I LOVE YOU BECAUSE...

_____
_____
_____
_____
_____
_____
_____
_____
_____
_____
_____
_____
_____

Draw the feeling...

_____
_____
_____
_____

Date:_____   Day #_____

I LOVE YOU BECAUSE...

_____
_____
_____
_____
_____
_____
_____
_____
_____
_____
_____
_____
_____
_____

Draw the feeling...

Date:_____   Day #_____

I LOVE YOU BECAUSE...

_____

_____

_____

_____

_____

_____

_____

_____

_____

_____

_____

_____

_____

_____

_____

Draw the feeling...

Date:_____ Day #_____

I LOVE YOU BECAUSE...

Draw the feeling...

Date:_____   Day #_____

I LOVE YOU BECAUSE...

_____

_____

_____

_____

_____

_____

_____

_____

_____

_____

_____

_____

_____

_____

_____

Draw the feeling...

_____

_____

_____

_____

_____

Date:_____   Day #_____

I LOVE YOU BECAUSE...

Draw the feeling...

Date:_____   Day #_____

I LOVE YOU BECAUSE...

_____
_____
_____
_____
_____
_____
_____
_____
_____
_____
_____
_____
_____
_____

Draw the feeling...

_____

Date:_____   Day #_____

I LOVE YOU BECAUSE...

_____
_____
_____
_____
_____
_____
_____
_____
_____
_____
_____
_____
_____
_____

Draw the feeling...

Date:_____ Day #_____

I LOVE YOU BECAUSE...

Draw the feeling...

Date:_____ Day #_____

I LOVE YOU BECAUSE...

Draw the feeling...

Date:_____   Day #_____

I LOVE YOU BECAUSE...

_____

_____

_____

_____

_____

_____

_____

_____

_____

_____

_____

_____

_____

Draw the feeling...

_____

_____

_____

_____

Date:_____ Day #_____

I LOVE YOU BECAUSE...

Draw the feeling...

Date:_____ Day #_____

I LOVE YOU BECAUSE...

_____

_____

_____

_____

_____

_____

_____

_____

_____

_____

_____

_____

_____

Draw the feeling...

_____

_____

_____

_____

_____

Date:_____ Day #_____

I LOVE YOU BECAUSE...

_____

_____

_____

_____

_____

_____

_____

_____

_____

_____

_____

_____

_____

_____

Draw the feeling...

_____

Date:_____   Day #_____

I LOVE YOU BECAUSE...

_____
_____
_____
_____
_____
_____
_____
_____
_____
_____
_____
_____
_____
_____
_____

Draw the feeling...

Date:_____ Day #_____

I LOVE YOU BECAUSE...

_____
_____
_____
_____
_____
_____
_____
_____
_____
_____
_____
_____
_____
_____

Draw the feeling...

Date:_____   Day #_____

I LOVE YOU BECAUSE...

_____

_____

_____

_____

_____

_____

_____

_____

_____

_____

_____

_____

_____

_____

Draw the feeling...

_____

_____

Date:_____ Day #_____

I LOVE YOU BECAUSE...

Draw the feeling...

Date:_____ Day #_____

I LOVE YOU BECAUSE...

_____
_____
_____
_____
_____
_____
_____
_____
_____
_____
_____
_____
_____
_____

Draw the feeling...

Date:_____ Day #_____

I LOVE YOU BECAUSE...

Draw the feeling...

Date:_____   Day #_____

I LOVE YOU BECAUSE...

_____

_____

_____

_____

_____

_____

_____

_____

_____

_____

_____

_____

_____

_____

Draw the feeling...

_____

_____

Date:_____   Day #_____

I LOVE YOU BECAUSE...

Draw the feeling...

Date:_____   Day #_____

I LOVE YOU BECAUSE...

_____

_____

_____

_____

_____

_____

_____

_____

_____

_____

_____

_____

_____

_____

Draw the feeling...

_____

Date:_____ Day #_____

I LOVE YOU BECAUSE...

_____
_____
_____
_____
_____
_____
_____
_____
_____
_____
_____
_____
_____
_____
_____
_____

Draw the feeling...

Date:_____   Day #_____

I LOVE YOU BECAUSE...

_____

_____

_____

_____

_____

_____

_____

_____

_____

_____

_____

_____

_____

_____   *Draw the feeling...*

_____

_____

_____

_____

_____

Date:_____   Day #_____

I LOVE YOU BECAUSE...

_____

_____

_____

_____

_____

_____

_____

_____

_____

_____

_____

_____

_____

_____

Draw the feeling...

_____

Date:_____   Day #_____

I LOVE YOU BECAUSE...

_____
_____
_____
_____
_____
_____
_____
_____
_____
_____
_____
_____
_____

Draw the feeling...

Date:_____   Day #_____

I LOVE YOU BECAUSE...

Draw the feeling...

Date:_____ Day #_____

I LOVE YOU BECAUSE...

_____

_____

_____

_____

_____

_____

_____

_____

_____

_____

_____

_____

_____

_____

_____

Draw the feeling...

_____

_____

_____

Date:_____   Day #_____

I LOVE YOU BECAUSE...

_____
_____
_____
_____
_____
_____
_____
_____
_____
_____
_____
_____
_____

Draw the feeling...

Date:_____   Day #_____

I LOVE YOU BECAUSE...

_____

_____

_____

_____

_____

_____

_____

_____

_____

_____

_____

_____

_____

_____

_____

Draw the feeling...

_____

Date:_____ Day #_____

I LOVE YOU BECAUSE...

Draw the feeling...

Date:_____   Day #_____

I LOVE YOU BECAUSE...

Draw the feeling...

Date:_____ Day #_____

I LOVE YOU BECAUSE...

Draw the feeling...

Date:_____   Day #_____

I LOVE YOU BECAUSE...

Draw the feeling...

Date:_____ Day #_____

I LOVE YOU BECAUSE...

Draw the feeling...

Made in the USA
Las Vegas, NV
20 March 2022

46001327R00057